PIANO ACCOMPANIMENT

Cathedral Music Press Presents

Sacred Melodies for Saxophone Solo

KEYBOARD ACCOMPANIMENT INCLUDED

By Mike Buerk

AF807828

Cathedral MUSIC PRESS

Contents

	B Flat Tenor Saxophone	E Flat Alto Saxophone	Piano
The Alto Saxophone (Preparatory Scale Studies)		14	
Amazing Grace	4	15	4
Christ the Lord Is Risen Today	5	16	6
Crown Him With Many Crowns	6	17	8
Faith Of Our Fathers	7	18	10
Holy, Holy, Holy	8	19	12
A Mighty Fortress Is Our God	9	20	14
Now Thank We All Our God	10	21	16
O Sacred Head, Now Wounded	11	22	18
Praise the Savior	12	23	20
The Tenor Saxophone (Preparatory Scale Studies)	3		

Amazing Grace

Arr. By Mike Buerk

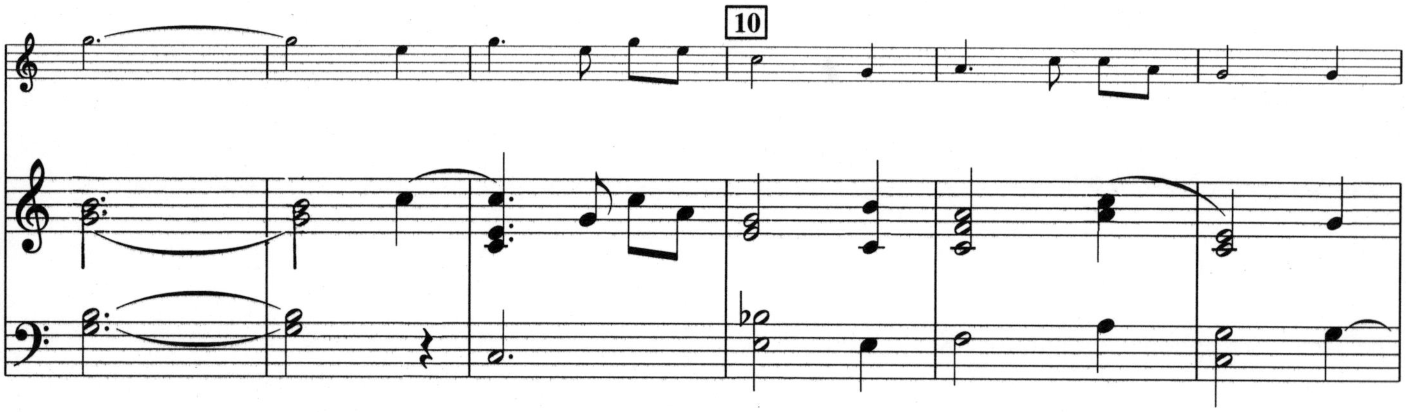

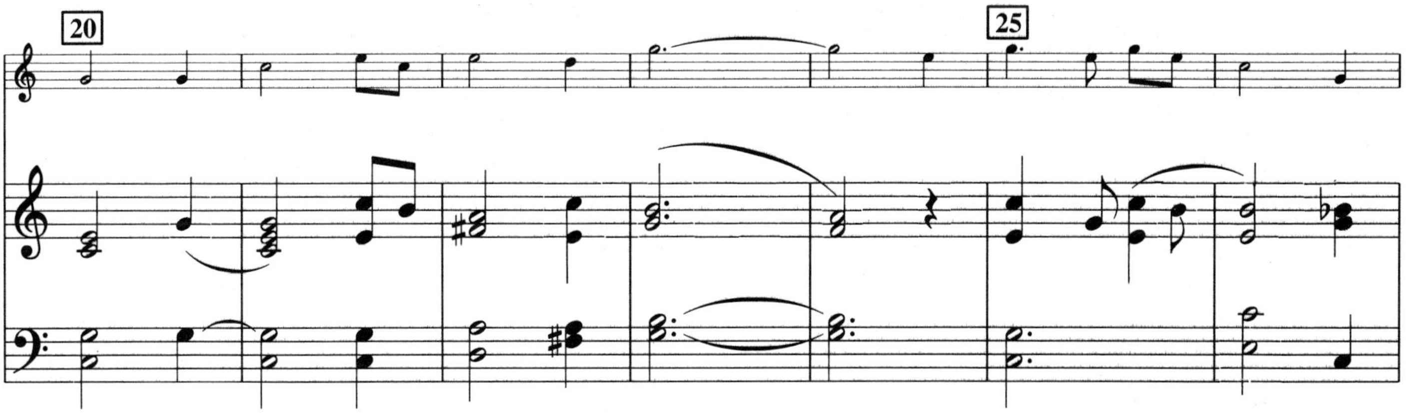
20
25

30

Christ The Lord Is Risen Today

Arr. By Mike Buerk

20
25
30

Crown Him With Many Crowns

By Mike Buerk

20
25
30

Faith Of Our Fathers

Arr. By Mike Buerk

30
35
40
45
8va

Holy, Holy, Holy

Arr. By Mike Buerk

15
20
25
30

A Mighty Fortress Is Our God

Arr. By Mike Buerk

20
25
30
35

Now Thank We All Our God

Arr. By Mike Buerk

25
30

O Sacred Head, Now Wounded

Arr. By Mike Buerk

15
20
25
30

Praise The Savior

Arr. By Mike Buerk